ADVICE TO YOUNG CHRISTIANS
EXPLORING PAUL'S LETTERS

**A 4-week course to
help junior highers
apply Paul's teachings
to their lives**

by Paul Woods

Group
Loveland, Colorado

Group

Advice to Young Christians: Exploring Paul's Letters
Copyright © 1992 Group Publishing, Inc.

Credits
Edited by Michael Warden
Cover designed by Diane Whisner
Illustrations by Raymond Medici
Cover photo by Brenda Rundback and David Priest

ISBN 1-55945-146-7
12 11 10 9 8 7 6 5 4   04 03 02 01 00 99 98 97 96
Printed in the United States of America.

CONTENTS

Advice to Young Christians: Exploring Paul's Letters

At Peace With God

Help junior highers grow more thankful for their relationship with God.

Humble Like Jesus

Help junior highers strive to be humble like Jesus.

In Good Hands

Help junior highers accept God's protection.

The Holy Spirit's Orchard

Help junior highers begin to let the Holy Spirit work through them.

ADVICE TO YOUNG CHRISTIANS: EXPLORING PAUL'S LETTERS

Abigail Van Buren and Ann Landers have been giving it for decades. Scores of magazines include it in every issue. Telephone hotlines offer it by the minute on topics ranging from sports to surgery—for a fee, of course.

Advice. It's something that's incredibly easy to give, but incredibly difficult to sift through.

Kids don't want pat answers dumped on them. They want to find real answers for themselves. They want answers that fit the difficult times as well as the good. They want answers that can help them understand themselves and their world.

Who Do Kids Listen To?

Here's how Christian teenagers rank the most important influences on their decisions about life's values:

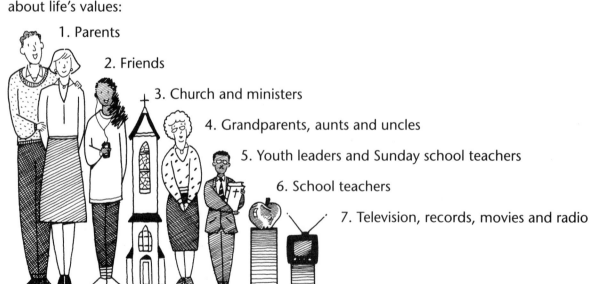

1. Parents
2. Friends
3. Church and ministers
4. Grandparents, aunts and uncles
5. Youth leaders and Sunday school teachers
6. School teachers
7. Television, records, movies and radio

Fortunately, kids are willing to listen to adults more readily than we sometimes think. A recent survey of Christian teenagers gave the results listed in the box below.

The good news is, church leaders rate above school teachers and television! So you do make an impact on your kids. And so will the advice of the Apostle Paul you'll study in this course.

After his life was changed when he met Jesus on the road to Damascus, Paul led an incredible life of service for God. He endured persecution and heartbreak, famine and abundance, shipwreck and stoning. He battled the established religious institution and brought thousands of outsiders to faith in Jesus.

The letters Paul wrote came out of his relationship with God. Inspired by the Holy Spirit, Paul gave his first-century readers advice to help them live God-pleasing Christian lives. And that advice still applies to us today.

As you use this course, you'll help your junior highers and middle schoolers get a better grasp on what the Christian life is all about. They'll learn why we want to live according to God's guidelines and why servanthood is so important. They'll also learn about God's protection and his work in their lives through his Holy Spirit.

In getting a taste of Paul's letters, kids will be encouraged to seek guidance from them as they face struggles in their lives. And kids will know they've got a heavenly Father and friend who's watching over them whatever happens.

By the end of this course, your students will
- understand how Jesus made it possible for them to be God's friends,
- see the need to be humble like Jesus,
- accept God's protection and
- begin to let the Holy Spirit work through them.

COURSE OBJECTIVES

HOW TO USE THIS COURSE

ACTIVE LEARNING

Think back on an important lesson you've learned in life. Did you learn it from reading about it? from hearing about it? from something you experienced? Chances are, the most important lessons you've learned came from something you experienced. That's what active learning is—learning by doing. And active learning is a key element in Group's Active Bible Curriculum™.

Active learning leads students in doing things that help them understand important principles, messages and ideas. It's a discovery process that helps kids internalize what they learn.

Each lesson section in Group's Active Bible Curriculum plays an important part in active learning:

The **Opener** involves kids in the topic in fun and unusual ways.

The **Action and Reflection** includes an experience designed to evoke specific feelings in the students. This section also processes those feelings through "How did you feel?" questions and applies the message to situations kids face.

The **Bible Application** actively connects the topic with the Bible. It helps kids see how the Bible is relevant to the situations they face.

The **Commitment** helps students internalize the Bible's message and commit to making changes in their lives.

The **Closing** funnels the lesson's message into a time of creative reflection and prayer.

When you put all the sections together, you get a lesson that's fun to teach. And kids get messages they'll remember.

BEFORE THE 4-WEEK SESSION

● Read the Introduction, the Course Objectives and This Course at a Glance.

● Decide how you'll publicize the course using the clip art on the Publicity Page (p. 9). Prepare fliers, newsletter articles and posters as needed.

● Look at the Bonus Ideas (p. 39) and decide which ones you'll use.

● Read the opening statements, Objectives and Bible Basis for the lesson. The Bible Basis shows how specific passages relate to junior highers and middle schoolers today.

● Choose which Opener and Closing options to use. Each is appropriate for a different kind of group.

● Gather necessary supplies from This Lesson at a Glance.

● Read each section of the lesson. Adjust where necessary for your class size and meeting room.

● The approximate minutes listed give you an idea of how long each activity will take. Each lesson is designed to take 35 to 60 minutes. Shorten or lengthen activities as needed to fit your group.

● If you see you're going to have extra time, do an activity or two from the "If You Still Have Time . . ." box or from the Bonus Ideas (p. 39).

● Dive into the activities with the kids. Don't be a spectator. The lesson will be more successful and rewarding to both you and your students.

● Though some kids may at first think certain activities are "silly," they'll enjoy them, and they'll remember the messages from these activities long after the lesson is over. As one Active Bible Curriculum user has said, "I can ask the kids questions about a lesson I did three weeks ago, and they actually remember what I taught!" And that's the whole idea of teaching . . . isn't it?

Have fun with the activities you lead. Remember, it is Jesus who encourages us to become "like little children." Besides, how often do your kids get *permission* to express their childlike qualities?

HELPFUL HINTS

● The answers given after discussion questions are responses your students *might* give. They aren't the only answers or the "right" answers. If needed, use them to spark discussion. Kids won't always say what you wish they'd say. That's why some of the responses given are negative or controversial. If someone responds negatively, don't be shocked. Accept the person and use the opportunity to explore other angles of the issue.

THIS COURSE AT A GLANCE

Before you dive into the lessons, familiarize yourself with each lesson aim. Then read the scripture passages.
- Study them as a background to the lessons.
- Use them as a basis for your personal devotions.
- Think about how they relate to kids' circumstances today.

LESSON 1: AT PEACE WITH GOD

Lesson Aim: To help junior highers grow more thankful for their relationship with God.

Bible Basis: Colossians 1:15-23.

LESSON 2: HUMBLE LIKE JESUS

Lesson Aim: To help junior highers strive to be humble like Jesus.

Bible Basis: Philippians 2:1-8.

LESSON 3: IN GOOD HANDS

Lesson Aim: To help junior highers accept God's protection.
Bible Basis: Ephesians 6:10-18.

LESSON 4: THE HOLY SPIRIT'S ORCHARD

Lesson Aim: To help junior highers begin to let the Holy Spirit work through them.

Bible Basis: Galatians 5:19-26.

PUBLICITY PAGE

Grab your junior highers' attention! Photocopy this page, and then cut out and paste the clip art of your choice in your church bulletin or newsletter to advertise this course on the Apostle Paul's advice for growing Christians. Or photocopy and use the ready-made flier as a bulletin insert. Permission to photocopy this clip art is granted for local church use.

Splash the clip art on posters, fliers or even postcards! Just add the vital details: the date and time the course begins and where you'll meet.

It's that simple.

ADVICE TO YOUNG CHRISTIANS
EXPLORING PAUL'S LETTERS

ADVICE TO YOUNG CHRISTIANS
EXPLORING PAUL'S LETTERS

Advice to Young Christians: Exploring Paul's Letters

A 4-week junior high and middle school course on applying the Apostle Paul's advice to your life

Come to _____

On _____

At _____

Come explore vital letters written to you over 1,500 years ago!

AT PEACE WITH GOD

Many junior highers and middle schoolers, even those who are Christians, tend to see God as a stern old man holding a club just waiting for them to step out of line. They see the fear of punishment as the reason for righteous living. Use this lesson to help kids see that living righteously is simply a grateful response to what God's done for us through Jesus.

LESSON AIM

To help junior highers grow more thankful for their relationship with God.

OBJECTIVES

Students will
- **experience peace after feeling frustrated, confused or frightened,**
- **experience the resolution of a conflict that seems unsolvable without violence,**
- **create a statement of what Jesus has done for them and**
- **commit themselves to living their lives in thankfulness to God.**

BIBLE BASIS
COLOSSIANS 1:15-23

Look up the following scripture. Then read the background paragraphs to see how the passage relates to your junior highers and middle schoolers.

In **Colossians 1:15-23,** Paul summarizes the importance of Christ to us.

Paul tells how Jesus was active in Creation, is head of the church and died on the cross. He explains to new believers how God has made it possible for us to be friends with him—to have a growing relationship with the God who made us.

Only through Jesus, and through our faith in him, can we

come before God. This is a message kids need to hear. Their lives should not be based on following a set of rules, but on thankfully seeking to please the one who made eternal life with God possible for all who believe.

THIS LESSON AT A GLANCE

Section	Minutes	What Students Will Do	Supplies
Opener (Option 1)	5 to 10	**Silent Peace**—Experience peace after a time of confusion.	Noisemakers
(Option 2)		**Terrified!**—Put themselves in the place of Jesus' disciples after Jesus' crucifixion.	
Action and Reflection	10 to 15	**The Fruit Solution**—Experience having someone make peace in a seemingly unsolvable conflict.	"Battle of Appearna" handouts (p. 17)
Bible Application	10 to 15	**Jesus in Action**—Determine what they would tell a teenage atheist about Jesus.	Bibles, paper, pencils
Commitment	5 to 10	**It's a Thankful Life**—Tell what it means to live lives of thankfulness to God.	Paper, pencils
Closing (Option 1)	5 to 10	**Our Awesome God**—Sing a contemporary song of praise or commitment and offer prayers of thanks.	Music, songbooks
(Option 2)		**We Thank You, God**—Offer responsive prayers for what God has done for us through Jesus.	

The Lesson

OPENER
(5 to 10 minutes)

☐ OPTION 1: SILENT PEACE

Before kids arrive, set up at least three noise-producing items and turn them on, such as a radio and a cassette player playing loudly and a vacuum cleaner running. The more noise, the better. Write on a chalkboard or newsprint, "Please sit down and be quiet."

As kids come in, point to the message and direct them to their seats. Let the noise continue for a couple of minutes. Make sure kids are completely quiet; then stop the noise all at once.

After kids express their relief, ask:

● **What do you like about having the noise stopped?** (It's nice and quiet; it's peaceful.)

● **Why do we like peace?** (It's the absence of conflict; it makes us more comfortable.)

Say: **It's frustrating when we want peace and can't seem to find it. Today we're going to be talking about the most important kind of peace we need—peace with God.**

☐ OPTION 2: TERRIFIED!

Tell kids you're going to set an imaginary scene for them, and they're to put themselves in it as you talk.

Say: **You're Jesus' original disciples. Three days ago you saw soldiers take Jesus away from you. You watched from a distance as the mob of people shouted for Jesus' crucifixion. You saw him hanging on the cross, dead. Rumors are flying around that the soldiers will come for Jesus' disciples next. You've also heard some people say Jesus has arisen, but you don't know if that could really be true. You're hiding out in a dark room, hoping you won't be found.**

Pause for a moment, then ask:

● **What are you feeling right now?** (Sorrow; fear; disappointment; confusion; terror.)

Then go on: **Suddenly Jesus appears next to you. He tells you, "Peace be with you." Then he shows you his hands and his side. You can see that he really is alive and well. His voice is reassuring, and he speaks with the same authority he always has.**

Ask:

● **How are you feeling now?** (Happy; excited; confident; at peace.)

● **Why do you now have peace that you didn't have before?** (Because Jesus is alive; because I know Jesus will be with me now.)

Say: **Jesus brought peace to his disciples that day. And he can bring peace to us, too. Through Jesus we can be at peace with God. We're going to talk about that peace today.**

THE FRUIT SOLUTION

Form two groups. Have one group go to another room, or at least go as far away as possible within your room. Give each person in one group a photocopy of the Country A section of the "Battle of Appearna" handout (p. 17). Give kids in the other group photocopies of the Country B section. Tell groups to read their handouts and that they have five minutes to come up with their plans.

After five minutes, bring the groups together and let Country A present its plan. Then let kids from Country B say what they don't like about the plan.

Let Country B present its plan and let kids from Country A say what they don't like about it.

When both groups have reported and responded, ask:

**A C T I O N A N D
R E F L E C T I O N**
(10 to 15 minutes)

● **What is the problem with both of these plans?** (They hurt people; they don't make everyone happy.)

● **Do you think there's any way to make everyone happy in this situation?** (No way; someone's got to lose.)

Say: **I think we may be missing something. Let me read the instructions given to each team.**

Read aloud both sets of instructions. Then say: **I think I have a solution. See what you think of it. Country A wants the appearna fruit for its seeds. Country B wants the fruit for everything but its seeds. Country A will send workers to Country B to cut the seeds out of the fruit. Then Country B will allow Country A to have the seeds free of charge to make medicine, and Country B will have the fruit to feed to its animals.**

Both countries wanted the same thing, but someone else had to provide a solution to make them both happy.
Ask:

● **How did it feel to discover there was a solution that could make you both happy? Explain.** (Great, I wasn't happy about killing everyone; mad, I wanted a big war.)

● **How was my providing a solution like what Jesus did for us when he died on the cross?** (God wanted us to have peace with him, and we wanted peace, too, but no one else could provide it; Jesus gave us the solution to our conflict.)

Say: **Through Jesus we can have a peaceful relationship with God that we couldn't have any other way. And because he's done that for us, we need to live our lives in thankfulness to him.**

BIBLE APPLICATION
(10 to 15 minutes)

JESUS IN ACTION

Form groups of three or four and give each person a sheet of paper and a pencil.

Say to the groups: **Someone you know at school claims to be an atheist, but lately he's been talking to you about who Jesus is. Using Colossians 1:15-23, work with your group members to put together a description of who Jesus is and what he has done. Then write one sentence telling your friend why you believe in Jesus.**

Give groups about 10 minutes, then have them report what they wrote. Ask:

● **Thinking about all the things you wrote in your descriptions of Jesus, how do those descriptions make you feel about Jesus?** (Grateful; loving; thankful.)

● **How do those things make you feel about your atheist friend? Explain.** (Sad that he doesn't know the truth; wishing I could convince her of the truth.)

● **If a person you know today did something to save you from certain death and crippled himself doing it, how would you act toward that person from now on?** (I'd be his servant; I'd do things to please him.)

Say: **Jesus has done so much for us. And we should do everything we can to express our thankfulness to him.**

IT'S A THANKFUL LIFE

Ask:

● **What can we do to thank Jesus for what he's done for us?** (Tell others about him; love God.)

Form pairs. Give each pair a sheet of paper and a pencil. Have partners work together to answer the following question on paper:

● **What does it mean to live our lives in thankfulness to God?**

Give kids about three minutes to answer the question. Encourage them to be as specific as possible. While kids are still in their pairs, have them report what they came up with.

Then say: **One way we can begin to live our lives in thankfulness to God is to treat others the way Jesus would treat them. Tell your partner one way you see him or her treating others the way they should be treated.**

After partners have shared, say: **Now, if you're really willing to commit yourself to living your life in thankfulness to God, sign the bottom of the paper you and your partner worked on. After class, I'll make photocopies so that each of you can have a copy.**

Be sure to make the photocopies and give them to the kids the following week.

COMMITMENT
(5 to 10 minutes)

Table Talk

The Table Talk activity in this course helps junior highers and middle schoolers talk with their parents about how to apply key teachings of the Apostle Paul to their lives.

If you choose to use the Table Talk activity, this is a good time to show students the "Table Talk" handout (p. 18). Ask them to spend time with their parents completing it.

Before kids leave, give them each a photocopy of the "Table Talk" handout to take home, or tell them you'll be sending it to their parents. Tell kids to be prepared to report on their experiences with the handout next week.

Or use the Table Talk idea found in the Bonus Ideas (p. 40) for a meeting based on the handout.

☐ OPTION 1: OUR AWESOME GOD

Have kids sing together a contemporary song of worship, praise or commitment, such as "Awesome God," "We Are the Reason" or "El Shaddai" from *The Group Songbook* (Group Books).

Close with prayer and encourage kids to offer prayers of personal commitment.

CLOSING
(5 to 10 minutes)

☐ OPTION 2: WE THANK YOU, GOD

Close with a responsive prayer. Begin the prayer by saying, "Thank you, Lord, for . . ." and then ask volunteers to say things they're thankful for. After each volunteer speaks, have the group repeat, "We thank you, God." Close the prayer by saying "amen" when you think kids are straining to think of things to say.

If You Still Have Time . . .

Powerful Practice—Form pairs and have kids tell each other what Christ has done for us. Encourage kids to add what Christ means to them personally.

Original Praise—Have small groups work together to write their own songs of praise related to thankfulness. Suggest the words be written to be sung to a familiar tune.

BATTLE OF APPEARNA

Cut apart the following directions for your teams.

COUNTRY A

Your country desperately needs appearna fruit. You've found that the seeds from the fruit can be dried, ground up and used to effectively combat a disease that's killing your country's livestock. The trouble is that appearna fruit grows in only one country, and that country wants to keep all its appearna fruit for its own use. Your goal is to think of a way—whatever it takes—to get that appearna fruit for your country.

COUNTRY B

Your country is the only country in the world that can grow appearna fruit. You use the fruit to feed your livestock, since normal grain won't grow in your country. But you have to cut the seeds out of the fruit because they make the animals sick. Another country wants your appearna fruit and your goal is to devise a way to protect your fruit no matter what the other country does to try to get it.

Table Talk

To the Parent: We're involved in a junior high course at church about the Apostle Paul's advice to young Christians. Students are exploring the Christian perspective Paul gave us for living as Christians. We'd like you and your teenager to spend some time discussing this important topic. Use this "Table Talk" page to help you do that.

Parent

Share with your teenager
- the most important advice you ever received.
- a passage from one of Paul's letters that has been particularly meaningful to you.
- a bit of advice you've been dying to give your teenager.

Junior higher

Share with your parent
- the best advice your parent has ever given you.
- the weakest advice your parent has ever given you.
- a bit of advice you've been dying to give your parent.

Parent and junior higher

- Read together Paul's brief explanation of the parent-child relationship in Ephesians 6:1-4.
- Discuss what it means to "obey," "honor" and "make angry."
- Tell one way you'll accept Paul's advice and treat the rest of your family in a more appropriate way.
- Choose one of Paul's smaller letters (such as Philippians), and read it during the coming week. Next week at this time, discuss what you discovered in your reading.

ADVICE TO YOUNG CHRISTIANS
EXPLORING PAUL'S LETTERS

HUMBLE LIKE JESUS

Junior highers and middle schoolers are not known for their humility. But Jesus was. Kids who tend to build themselves up by putting others down need to realize that Jesus' way of doing things was exactly the opposite—Jesus built himself up by serving and caring for others.

To help junior highers strive to be humble like Jesus.

LESSON AIM

Students will
- **experience acting proud,**
- **play roles that express pride,**
- **evaluate and revise roles to express humility and**
- **commit to doing at least one humble act this week.**

OBJECTIVES

Look up the following scripture. Then read the background paragraphs to see how the passage relates to your junior highers and middle schoolers.

In **Philippians 2:1-8,** Paul describes Jesus' attitude of humility.

In this passage, Paul describes how Jesus—who is God—humbled himself to become a human, to be a servant of other common humans and to die an undeserved death on the cross for the sake of humans.

Jesus' humility is an example for all of us. When we're tempted to think we're pretty important, we need to be reminded of Jesus' attitude. Kids need to realize that making oneself look important in human eyes will do little but make one look less important to God. Indeed, we must put aside our own desires for power and prestige and "be interested in the lives of others"—like Christ Jesus.

BIBLE BASIS
PHILIPPIANS 2:1-8

Section	Minutes	What Students Will Do	Supplies
Opener (Option 1)	5 to 10	**The Test**—Receive imaginary test papers to be proud of.	Paper, marker
(Option 2)		**Humility Standing**—Stand on a continuum to indicate their willingness to do unpleasant tasks.	Posterboard, marker, tape
Action and Reflection	15 to 20	**Too Many Chiefs**—Simulate being marooned on an island with people who all think they're important.	"Culligan's Island Roles" handouts (p. 24), "Culligan's Island" handouts (p. 25)
Bible Application	5 to 10	**Return to Culligan's Island**—Revise their roles from the last activity to reflect Christ's humility.	Bibles, paper, pencils
Commitment	5 to 10	**Humility Is**—List specific tasks they're asked to do that they hate doing—and commit to doing one this week.	Chalkboard and chalk, or newsprint and marker
Closing (Option 1)	5 to 10	**Prayer of St. Francis**—Listen to the prayer of one of God's humble servants.	Cassette player, recording of or words for the "Prayer of St. Francis"
(Option 2)		**List Prayer**—Pray through the actions listed earlier and ask for God's help in doing them.	

The Lesson

OPENER
(5 to 10 minutes)

☐ OPTION 1: THE TEST

Before class, make up enough "test papers" for all your kids by writing a test score at the top of each sheet of paper. Put high scores, such as 95 and 100, on about half of the papers and put low scores, such as 60 or 65, on the other half. Don't give letter grades.

As class begins, say: **You've just taken an imaginary test. Anyone doing well on this test will likely become a doctor or a lawyer. Anyone flunking this test will likely end up jobless and homeless. Here are your test scores.**

Hand out the papers at random. Give kids a minute to look at and compare their papers. Some will probably gloat over their high scores.

Then ask:

● **How did it feel to get a high score on the test?** (Great; I didn't care.)

● **How did it feel to get a low score?** (I was upset; it really didn't matter.)

Then say: **Wait! Did I tell you that the high scores were** best? Oh, no! I meant the opposite. Everyone with a 65 or below will be the doctors and lawyers. If you got a 90 or higher, you'll probably end up on the street.

Kids who thought they did poorly but actually did well will now do the gloating.

Ask:

● **Now, how did it feel to get a low score? Explain.** (Great; it was good to know I did better than those kids who thought they were so great.)

● **How is the way you acted when you thought you had a good score like the way some people act in life?** (Some people think they're so smart, even though they really aren't; some kids think they're better than anyone else.)

Say: **Part of what we've been talking about is called pride. It's the tendency to lift ourselves up because we think we're really good at something. But that attitude is one that Jesus rejected. Today we're going to look at the kind of attitude Jesus had.**

☐ OPTION 2: HUMILITY STANDING

Before the meeting, use posterboard and a marker to make two signs, one that says "Anytime I'm asked" and the other, "Never in a million years." Tape the signs at opposite ends of the room.

As kids arrive, tell them you're going to describe some tasks they might be asked to do. Tell them they're each to stand at a spot somewhere between the two signs to indicate how willing they would be to do what you asked.

Read the following actions aloud one at a time and let kids move to the spot on the continuum that best represents their willingness to do that task. After each action, ask volunteers to share why they chose their particular spot. Here are the actions:

● **Take out the garbage.**

● **Babysit for free so a single mom in your neighborhood can go shopping.**

● **Clean up after your sister when she gets sick with the flu.**

● **Wash dinner dishes by yourself.**

● **Clean your gender's restrooms at school.**

After going through all the actions, ask:

● **All of these tasks need to be done by someone. Why do so few of us want to do them?** (We're too proud; nobody likes that stuff.)

Say: **There are a lot of things many of us are too proud to do. But that wasn't the attitude Jesus had. Even though he was God, he became a servant. And he wants us to have that kind of attitude, too. Today we're going to talk about humility.**

Table Talk Follow-Up

If you sent the "Table Talk" handout (p. 18) to parents last week, discuss students' reactions to the activity. Ask volunteers to share what they learned from the discussion with their parents.

ACTION AND REFLECTION

(15 to 20 minutes)

TOO MANY CHIEFS

Before class, make one photocopy of the "Culligan's Island Roles" handout (p. 24) for every five students. Cut apart the instructions for the various roles, keeping them in complete sets of five different roles.

Form groups of five. Give each group one of the sets and have kids randomly distribute the instructions in their groups. It's okay if you have fewer than five kids for the last group you form. Just hand out fewer role instructions.

Say: **Think about your role and how the person you're playing might act in the situation. Put yourself into the role.**

Now give each person a "Culligan's Island" handout (p. 25). Have kids read through it in their groups. Have kids role play for seven minutes to divide up the duties. Then discuss the following questions.

● **What made it difficult to get the tasks assigned?** (No one wanted to do the dirty jobs; everyone wanted to be boss.)

● **How did the roles you played affect your attitudes?** (I didn't want to do menial jobs; I was too smart to wash dishes.)

● **How did it feel to be assigned a dirty job when you were an important person?** (I hated it; it wasn't fair.)

● **How is this like the way others sometimes act in real life?** (People think they're too good for certain jobs; kids think they're hot stuff.)

● **How is this like the way we sometimes act?** (We think we're pretty cool sometimes; we think we're too good for certain things.)

Say: **Humility doesn't come easily. But Jesus, who deserved to be treated as God, gave us an example of humility that we should all strive to follow. Let's look at that example now.**

BIBLE APPLICATION

(5 to 10 minutes)

RETURN TO CULLIGAN'S ISLAND

Have kids remain in the same groups as the last activity. Give each group a sheet of paper and a pencil and have groups read Philippians 2:1-8.

Say: **Now let's go back to Culligan's Island. Using this scripture passage as a guide, discuss in your group how your character might offer to do the tasks required if following Christ's example. Assign one person in your group to jot down some of your ideas to report later.**

Give kids about five minutes, then call them together to report. Have groups each tell how the characters would act differently if following Christ's example.

HUMILITY IS

Say: **We've talked a lot about humility, but what does it really mean in our lives. What kinds of things would a humble junior higher or middle schooler do?**

List kids' responses on a chalkboard or newsprint. Ask kids to be specific about actions they'd do. After you have at least 15 things listed, have kids form pairs.

Say: **From the list we've made, choose one thing you'll commit yourself to do in the next week. Tell your partner what it is and why you chose it.**

Give kids a minute to choose their actions and tell their partners. Then say: **Now, before you leave your partner, tell him or her one reason you admire the commitment he or she made to be more humble.**

When kids are finished, draw them back together for your closing.

☐ OPTION 1: PRAYER OF ST. FRANCIS

If you have access to a recording of the "Prayer of St. Francis," play it and ask kids to quietly meditate on the words. If you don't have a recording of the song, read it as a poem while kids listen quietly. If you have photocopies of it, have kids read it together as a closing prayer.

Close with a simple "amen."

☐ OPTION 2: LIST PRAYER

Form a circle. Using the list of humble actions you made in the Humility Is activity, go around the circle and have kids pray, asking God to help all of you be more humble in the specific areas kids mentioned. Close by asking God to help all of you exhibit humility in the way Christ did in humbling himself to die for us on the cross.

COMMITMENT
(5 to 10 minutes)

CLOSING
(5 to 10 minutes)

If You Still Have Time . . .

Animal Humbleness—Have kids each name the animal they think is the most humble and explain why. Then have them suggest how they could be more like that animal.

Definition of Humility—Have kids look up "humility" in a concordance or topical index of the Bible. Then, after looking up the passages listed there, let kids work together to write a definition of humility that fits teenagers' lives today.

CULLIGAN'S ISLAND ROLES

Culligan's Island
Role A

Your group is marooned on an island. You're suspicious that there may be dangerous wildlife on the island. You don't know how long it will take to be rescued, so you have to figure out a way to function as a group to stay alive.

You are a NASA scientist heavily involved in the development of a new space-station concept. Your IQ is well into the genius range. You're pretty proud of who you are and what you've done.

Culligan's Island
Role B

Your group is marooned on an island. You're suspicious that there may be dangerous wildlife on the island. You don't know how long it will take to be rescued, so you have to figure out a way to function as a group to stay alive.

You are one of the wealthiest people in the world. You have billions in bank accounts in Europe. You own yachts, a private jet and seven different mansions around the world. You're pretty proud of who you are and what you've done.

Culligan's Island
Role C

Your group is marooned on an island. You're suspicious that there may be dangerous wildlife on the island. You don't know how long it will take to be rescued, so you have to figure out a way to function as a group to stay alive.

You're a five-star general. You've been in charge of thousands of soldiers and have had hundreds of officers carrying out your orders. You're pretty proud of who you are and what you've done.

Culligan's Island
Role D

Your group is marooned on an island. You're suspicious that there may be dangerous wildlife on the island. You don't know how long it will take to be rescued, so you have to figure out a way to function as a group to stay alive.

You're an Internal Revenue Service agent. People cower when they find out what you do. You've put away hundreds of people for cheating on their taxes, and you have trouble making friends because of your job. You're pretty proud of who you are and what you've done.

Culligan's Island
Role E

Your group is marooned on an island. You're suspicious that there may be dangerous wildlife on the island. You don't know how long it will take to be rescued, so you have to figure out a way to function as a group to stay alive.

You're a tennis champion. You've won at Wimbledon three times, and most everyone in the world recognizes you. You enjoy all the attention you get. You're pretty proud of who you are and what you've done.

CULLIGAN'S ISLAND

Your task is to divide up the following duties. They can be divided up in any way. No one person has to do all of one duty. Remember to stay in your role as you work in your groups.

A. 24-hour guard duty (protecting the group against wild animals; watching for ships)

B. Hunting and gathering (searching for edible berries and roots; catching fish or small animals)

C. Food preparation (cleaning and preparing whatever food is found)

D. Sanitation (digging a latrine; taking care of it daily)

E. Shelter and rescue (building a shelter for each gender; devising a way to be rescued)

F. Laundry (washing clothes)

G. Cleanup (cleaning up after meals; keeping shelters tidy)

H. Supervision (leading the group and making sure jobs get done)

LESSON 3

IN GOOD HANDS

Middle schoolers are often tempted to believe they're invincible. They're young and strong, and life looms before them like a great adventure ready to be experienced. But there are real dangers—from both inside and outside their world—that kids face. Only with God's help can they truly overcome.

LESSON AIM

To help junior highers accept God's protection.

OBJECTIVES

Students will
- think about what it means to be protected,
- attempt to protect someone from a physical attack,
- compare firefighters' armor to the spiritual armor God offers us and
- share a symbol of spiritual armor with another student.

BIBLE BASIS
EPHESIANS 6:10-18

Look up the following scripture. Then read the background paragraphs to see how the passage relates to your junior highers and middle schoolers.

In **Ephesians 6:10-18,** Paul describes the armor God provides for us to put on to protect us from Satan's attacks.

Though we tend to ignore it, there's a real spiritual battle going on around us—and sometimes inside of us! But God provides protection from whatever the enemy can throw at us, if we depend on God and use the armor he's given us.

Kids, just like adults, sometimes think they can do things on their own without looking to God for help or protection. When that happens, we're all sorry. This passage will encourage kids to put on God's armor and take a stand in the battle they're facing.

Section	Minutes	What Students Will Do	Supplies
Opener (Option 1)	5 to 10	**The Shepherd**—Roam around like sheep and be protected by a shepherd.	
(Option 2)		**Deep-Sea Protection**—Imagine the protection needed for a dive into shark-infested waters.	Chalkboard and chalk or newsprint and marker
Action and Reflection	15 to 20	**Attack of the Killer Marshmallows**—Create protection for a group member to prevent "wounding" by a marshmallow.	Newspapers, masking tape, marshmallows
Bible Application	10 to 15	**Fighting Fire**—Create a firefighter's "armor" based on the spiritual armor God gives us.	Bibles, a box of old clothes, markers, posterboard, scissors
Commitment	5 to 10	**Armor to Go**—Share a piece of the armor they created as a reminder of God's armor.	Armor created in the Attack of the Killer Marshmallows activity, scissors
Closing (Option 1)	up to 5	**Armed With the Word**—Write a prayer to God based on today's passage.	Bible, 3×5 cards, pencils, pins or tape
(Option 2)		**By His Spirit**—Draw images related to God's protection.	Paper, colored markers

The Lesson

☐ OPTION 1: THE SHEPHERD

After kids arrive, ask for a volunteer to be a shepherd. Tell everyone how important the shepherd's job is in protecting the sheep. Then have the rest of the kids get down on all fours and roam around the room making sheep noises.

Say: **Pretend you're out on a hill eating grass when suddenly a mountain lion leaps from a ledge above you and races for one of the sheep. Quick, shepherd, what do you do?**

Keep pressing the shepherd for an answer that somehow involves protecting the sheep. Have the shepherd act out the answer. Then say: **The sheep are safe from the mountain lion, but suddenly there's a crack of lightning nearby. A big storm is almost upon you. Quick, shepherd, what do you do?**

Again, press for an answer that involves protecting the sheep. After the shepherd acts out the answer, say: **The storm is over, the danger is past, but now it's getting late. You dare not be out on the open plain at night because wild**

OPENER
(5 to 10 minutes)

animals will come from all around you. Quick, shepherd, what do you do?

Once more, press for an answer indicating protection of the sheep. After the shepherd and sheep act out the answer, thank everyone for participating and have them sit down.

Ask:

● **What did the shepherd do for the sheep?** (Protected them; gave them shelter.)

● **How is this like the way God protects us?** (He gets us out of trouble; he provides what we need.)

Say: **Today we're going to be looking at how God protects us from spiritual dangers and how we can trust in that protection.**

OPTION 2: DEEP-SEA PROTECTION

After kids arrive, say: **Suppose you're going on a deep-sea treasure hunt. You're going down to search for sunken treasure in shark- and barracuda-infested waters. What do you need to take with you?**

Have kids list things to take. Write their responses on a chalkboard or newsprint. Kids' list should include items such as a diving cage to protect them from sharks, spear guns, plenty of oxygen and a protective wetsuit.

Ask:

● **Why do you need all that stuff?** (To protect me from sharks; to stay alive.)

● **How is that protection like the protection we need in our spiritual lives?** (We need to be protected from Satan; we don't always know what dangers are out there.)

Say: **Today we're going to talk about how God protects us in the midst of the spiritual dangers we face.**

ATTACK OF THE KILLER MARSHMALLOWS

Form groups of four or five. Station the groups around the room, apart from each other. Have the person in each group whose birthday is closest to today become the "Protected." Give groups lots of newspapers and masking tape and tell them to use the papers and tape to "protect" their Protected from an attack of marshmallows. Tell them that no part of the body should be vulnerable to a marshmallow attack.

Give kids about five minutes to make a shelter or armor to protect their Protected. When all groups are ready, say: **I'm going to give each person, except for the Protecteds, one marshmallow. You are to try to "wound" another team's Protected by hitting him or her with a marshmallow on the skin or clothing. You must stay at least 6 feet away from a person to throw your marshmallow, and you may throw it only once.**

Hand out the marshmallows and give kids the "go" signal. Be sure to stop the action quickly after each person has thrown his or her marshmallow. Go around and judge the "safety" of each group's Protected. Then have kids unwrap the Protecteds and all join together.

Ask:

● **Protecteds, how did it feel to be under attack?** (Weird, I couldn't even see; fun, I knew I was safe.)

● **How effective was your protection?** (Great, no marks; not so good.)

● **Was one type of protection better than another? Why or why not?** (Yes, ours was best because it worked; no, some kids just got lucky.)

● **How was this experience like the way God protects us from spiritual attacks?** (His protection is a lot better; he saves us from a lot worse things than marshmallows.)

Say: **How well we're protected depends on our armor. That's similar to God's protection. How well God is able to protect us depends on how much of his armor we choose to wear each day. Next we're going to look at a passage of scripture that will help us understand God's armor better.**

FIGHTING FIRE

Before the meeting, gather together a boxful of old clothes, such as shirts, pants, shoes and hats. Also collect markers, posterboard and scissors.

Have kids turn to Ephesians 6:10-13. Ask a volunteer to read the passage aloud.

Then say: **The rest of this passage is probably familiar to you. But today we're going to take a little different look at it. We're going to compare the armor listed here to a firefighter's armor.**

Form three groups. A group can be one person. Assign each group one of the following passages: Ephesians 6:14; 6:15-16; and 6:17. Bring out the box of old clothes and the markers, posterboard and scissors.

Say: **Read through your verse or verses and create from the materials here a piece of firefighter's equipment that compares to the spiritual armor in your passage. Be sure to write on it the name of the spiritual armor piece it re-presents.**

Give groups about five minutes to create their firefighter's armor. Then select one volunteer to model all the armor. He or she should leave it on for the rest of this activity. Have groups each explain the piece they created.

Then ask:

● **How does each piece of spiritual armor help us?**

Go through each piece listed in the passage, having kids suggest ways the piece of armor helps them in real life. Encourage kids to be specific.

When you've finished with verses 14 through 17, read aloud Ephesians 6:18.

BIBLE APPLICATION
(10 to 15 minutes)

Ask:
● **How does this added element of protection help us?**
(Gives us contact with the one who can help; it's like a fire-fighter's water hose.)

Say: **With all this protection, we ought to be in pretty good shape! But sometimes we set out on our own without all the protection. And then we get into trouble. We need to learn to constantly lean on God for his protection and not go our own way.**

ARMOR TO GO

Have your model take off the armor and have kids get back into the groups they were just in. Give each group the piece of armor they created and a pair of scissors.

Say: **Now cut a small piece of your armor piece for each person in your group. Make each piece no bigger than 2×2 inches.**

Give kids a minute to make their small pieces. Then say: **Now, one at a time, turn to the person on your right and give him or her your piece of the armor as you say, "Here is a piece of God's armor to remind you to rely on him." Then tell that person one reason why he or she is valuable and worth protecting. For example, you might say "You're worth protecting because you're a good listener." Make sure your comments are positive.**

After kids have gone around their groups, encourage them to take their armor pieces home with them to help them remember that God's armor is there for them every day.

☐ OPTION 1: ARMED WITH THE WORD

Form a circle and read aloud Ephesians 6:10-18, pausing after each verse.

Give kids each a 3×5 card and a pencil and have them each write a short personal prayer of protection to God based on the passage. When everyone is finished, encourage kids to pin or tape their prayers to their armor pieces.

☐ OPTION 2: BY HIS SPIRIT

Give kids paper and colored markers and have them each draw a picture or symbol that represents God's constant protection in their lives.

When kids are finished, ask them to pray silently for God to help them realize the true depth of his protection and love. After a few moments, close with a brief prayer of thanks. Encourage kids to keep their drawings with their armor pieces as a reminder of God's ever-present protection for them.

COMMITMENT
(5 to 10 minutes)

CLOSING
(up to 5 minutes)

If You Still Have Time . . .

Protection Wanted—Have kids list specific things they feel they need protection from, such as pressure to drink or temptation to cheat. Once you have a good list, let kids suggest ways God can protect them against each thing on the list.

The Great Protector—Have kids work in small groups to create stories or comic strips showing how God came through to protect someone in tough circumstances.

LESSON 4

THE HOLY SPIRIT'S ORCHARD

Kids today know what it's like to be self-ish. And, even if teenagers don't center their every activity around personal, selfish desires, they certainly know a couple dozen kids who do! But following our own selfish wants won't bring happiness to or strengthen our relationship with God. Use this lesson to help your kids see the benefit of letting the Holy Spirit work to produce lasting, unselfish fruit in their lives.

LESSON AIM

To help junior highers begin to let the Holy Spirit work through them.

OBJECTIVES

Students will
- compare fruit that comes from specific trees to fruit in their lives,
- experience being led to something good or bad,
- examine the fruit produced by the sinful self and by the Holy Spirit and
- apply the fruit of the Spirit to situations in their daily lives.

BIBLE BASIS
GALATIANS 5:19-26

Look up the following scripture. Then read the background paragraphs to see how the passage relates to your junior highers and middle schoolers.

In **Galatians 5:19-26,** Paul contrasts the fruit of the sinful self and the fruit of the Spirit.

When we serve our selfish desires, we end up with all sorts of problems. Sexual promiscuity has several well-known undesirable results. Witchcraft, uncontrolled anger, jealousy and alcohol abuse carry their own particular poisons. And all of them threaten a person's stability in the kingdom of God.

But serving the Holy Spirit produces a different kind of fruit—fruit that will bring happiness to ourselves and those around us. Fruit that comes naturally when we follow Christ and seek the Spirit's working in our lives.

Kids need to see that the self-serving attitudes so prevalent today will lead only to pain. And that serving the Spirit will lead them to ultimate joy in their relationship with God—and in their lives.

THIS LESSON AT A GLANCE

Section	Minutes	What Students Will Do	Supplies
Opener (Option 1)	5 to 10	**By Their Fruit**—Identify the trees that different fruits come from by smelling and feeling the fruits.	Fruits, paper grocery sack
(Option 2)		**Cars Is Not Cars**—Discuss why certain models of cars come only from certain automakers.	Chalkboard and chalk or newsprint and marker
Action and Reflection	10 to 15	**The Mean Leading the Blind**—Lead or be led to something good or something bad.	Blindfolds, posterboard, marker
Bible Application	15 to 20	**Whose Fruit?**—Make warning labels for the fruit of the sinful self and for the fruit of the Spirit.	Bibles, paper, pencils
Commitment	5 to 10	**Our Daily Fruit**—Write how the fruit of the Spirit applies to our daily lives.	Chalkboard and chalk or newsprint and markers
Closing (Option 1)	up to 5	**Apple of His Eye**—Receive an apple and an encouragement to let the Spirit bear fruit in their lives.	Apples
(Option 2)		**Fruit That Shows**—Share a piece of "fruit" with a partner and with the group.	Construction paper squares, pencils

The Lesson

☐ OPTION 1: BY THEIR FRUIT

Before class, gather four different kinds of fruit in a paper grocery sack, such as an apple, a pear, an orange and a banana.

Say: **I have four pieces of fruit in this bag, and you're**

OPENER
(5 to 10 minutes)

going to guess what kind of tree each piece came from. But you have to do it with your eyes shut tightly.

Have kids stand in a line and tell them to close their eyes. Begin passing the fruit down the line one at a time. Kids may feel and smell each piece of fruit but must keep their eyes closed until everyone is done. Instruct kids to keep quiet and remember which piece of fruit was first, second, third and fourth.

After all the kids have felt the fruit, put it back in the bag and tell kids to open their eyes. Ask what kind of tree the first, second, third and fourth pieces of fruit came from. Kids should have no trouble figuring out the fruits.

Say: **Even with your eyes closed, it wasn't tough to tell what kind of tree each fruit came from. Fruit from each type of tree has readily identifiable characteristics.**

Ask:
● **If there was a "Christian" tree, what would be the characteristics of fruit coming from it?** (Honesty; kindness; love.)

Say: **Today we're going to talk about the fruit that shows naturally in Christians when they let the Holy Spirit live and work in them.**

☐ OPTION 2: CARS IS NOT CARS

Ask kids to name some major auto manufacturers. Write their responses across the top of a chalkboard or newsprint, to serve as column heads. When you've listed four or five manufacturers, have kids list models of cars made by each of these manufacturers. Write each car model under the appropriate heading. If possible, have kids run out to a nearby parking lot to find a variety of models to add to the list.

After you've listed four or five models under each heading, ask the following question using a car and a manufacturer from the list:
● **Why don't we see a** (model of car) **being made by** (name of manufacturer)? (Because Chevrolet doesn't make Fords; they make their own cars.)

Ask the same question a couple more times using different cars and car makers in the question. Then say: **We know that each model of car is identified as coming from a particular maker. That's kind of how it is with people. The things we do and the way we act identify who is at work in our lives. Today we're going to be looking at what it means to have the Holy Spirit working in us.**

THE MEAN LEADING THE BLIND

Before class, use posterboard and a marker to make two signs: one saying "water," the other saying "mirage."

Form two groups. Blindfold one group. After the blindfolds are on, put the "water" sign at one end of the room and the "mirage" sign at the other end. Don't let the blindfolded kids know which is which.

ACTION AND REFLECTION
(10 to 15 minutes)

Have the remaining half of your class form two equal groups. Say to one of the groups: **You're the good guys. You're each going to find some soul wandering blindly in the desert and lead the person to water.**

To the other group, say: **You're the bad guys. You're each going to find some soul wandering blindly in the desert and lead the person to a mirage.**

Tell the blindfolded kids to start silently wandering around the room. Have the other kids each silently find a blindfolded person and lead him or her to the appropriate end of the room.

When all kids are at one end of the room or the other, have kids take off the blindfolds and see where they're at.

Ask:

● **How did it feel being led by someone you didn't know was good or bad? Explain.** (Anxious, I didn't know where I was going; exciting, it was an adventure.)

● **How is this like the way we're sometimes led by others in life?** (We don't always know who's good to follow; sometimes we think we're right but we're not.)

● **How important is it to be able to trust the person who's leading us? Explain.** (Very, otherwise we could be in big trouble; not so important, we can find our way anyway.)

● **What would it be like to be led by the Holy Spirit in our lives? Explain.** (Great, the Holy Spirit helps us know what to do; I'm not sure, I don't know if it would be fun.)

● **How was this experience like or unlike letting the Holy Spirit lead us?** (It's just like it because we can trust God even if we don't know where we're going; it's not the same because God never leads us to bad things.)

Say: **When the Holy Spirit is leading us—and we're following the Holy Spirit—we can depend on the Holy Spirit leading us into good things. And the things that happen in our lives will also be good for others. Let's take a look at the kind of fruit the Holy Spirit produces in our lives.**

WHOSE FRUIT?

Form groups of three or four. Give each group a sheet of paper and a pencil. Assign half of the groups Galatians 5:19-21. Assign the other half Galatians 5:22-26.

Say: **Each group is to create a warning label for the type of fruit talked about in your passage. The Galatians 5:19-21 groups will create a label for the fruit of the sinful self. This label should describe the "contents" of the fruit and the risks or dangers of the fruit. The Galatians 5:22-26 groups will create a label for the fruit of the Spirit. This label should also describe the "contents" of the fruit as well as the risks. Make sure your label clearly spells out the dangers involved with each kind of fruit.**

Give groups about seven minutes to read their passages and create their labels. Then read both passages aloud and

BIBLE APPLICATION
(15 to 20 minutes)

have all groups present their labels.

When all groups have reported, ask:

● **What produces the fruit of the Spirit?** (The Holy Spirit; following Jesus.)

● **How can the good qualities in the fruit of the Spirit be helpful in your lives and relationships?** (They can help me make friends; they help me deal with frustrating times.)

● **How can we have the Holy Spirit working in our lives?** (By living for Jesus; by giving up our selfishness.)

If kids have trouble answering the last question, refer them to Galatians 5:24-25.

Say: **Notice that these good qualities don't come because we are good. They come because we say yes to God's Spirit working in us. Just like an apple tree naturally produces apples, a Christian with the Spirit working through him or her naturally produces the fruit of the Spirit. And while the fruit of the flesh needs an extensive warning label, the fruit of the Spirit needs no warning at all!**

OUR DAILY FRUIT

Say: **Now let's see how we can begin to produce the fruit of the Spirit in our own lives.**

Write each of the qualities of the fruit of the Spirit from Galatians 5:22-23 across the top of a chalkboard or on separate sheets of newsprint around the room.

Say: **The fruit of the Spirit should show up in our daily lives if we're living in a growing relationship with God. Under each quality listed here, write one specific way you will show that fruit of the Spirit in your life. For example, under patience you might write, "Don't hassle my sister because she takes too long in the bathroom."**

Have kids start at different places and write something under each quality. If you have more than 12 kids, have them each write under only four or five qualities.

Discuss together what kids have written.

☐ OPTION 1: APPLE OF HIS EYE

Get out a bag of apples and have kids stand quietly in a circle. From inside the circle, go to each individual and as you hand him or her an apple, say: (Name), **you are the apple of God's eye. Let his Holy Spirit produce fruit in you.**

Close with prayer, asking God to help your kids be open to the working of the Holy Spirit in their lives.

After the prayer, eat the apples together as a symbol of letting God's Holy Spirit come and fill each person.

☐ OPTION 2: FRUIT THAT SHOWS

Form pairs. Give kids each a 4-inch square of construction paper and a pencil. Say: **Tear your paper into the shape of**

a piece of fruit and write on it one way you see the fruit of the Spirit showing up in your partner's life.

When kids are ready, form a circle and have kids each explain their piece of fruit as they give it to their partner. Close with prayer, allowing volunteers to pray for the fruit of the Spirit to show in their lives.

If You Still Have Time . . .

Sowing Seeds—Take a look at the list of fruit in Galatians 5:22-23 and have kids come up with a "seed" for each fruit—an attitude that eventually leads to the fruit. For example, a seed for love might be an attitude of unselfishness. Several of the qualities may come from a similar seed.

Course Reflection—Form a circle. Ask students to reflect on the past four lessons. Have them take turns completing the following sentences:

● Something I learned in this course is . . .

● If I could tell my friends about this course, I'd say . . .

● Something I'll do differently because of this course is . . .

BONUS IDEAS

Bonus Scriptures—The lessons focus on a select few scripture passages, but if you'd like to incorporate more of Paul's teachings into the lessons, here are our suggestions:

● Romans 6:1-14 (Paul writes about our new life in Christ through Christ's death and resurrection.)

● Romans 12:1-2 (Paul charges Christians to give their lives to God as a living sacrifice.)

● 1 Corinthians 12:14-27 (Paul discusses spiritual gifts.)

● 1 Corinthians 13:1-13 (Paul describes the nature of true love.)

● 1 Thessalonians 5:1-11 (Paul talks about Jesus' return.)

● 1 Timothy 6:11-16 (Paul encourages Christians to run from evil and live for God.)

Who Is Paul, Anyway?—Take time to learn about Paul and how he viewed his own life. Use Philippians 3:1-14 as a guide, and pull highlights from Acts 9—28.

Spiritual Fitness—Have kids dress in workout gear and examine spiritual fitness as described in 1 Corinthians 9:24-27. Compare various types of physical exercise to spiritual "exercises" that help us become more spiritually fit and draw closer in our relationship with God.

Police Protection—Arrange a visit to a local police headquarters. Ask an officer to explain how the department works to protect the citizens of your area. After your visit, compare how the police department works with how God works. Also discuss the purpose and effectiveness of both kinds of protection.

Friends With God—Examine more of what it means to be reconciled to God. Good passages to use are 2 Corinthians 5:11—6:2 and Ephesians 2:11-22.

Humble Characters—Learn more about biblical humility by looking at some of the Bible's most humble characters. Check out Exodus 3:1-12; Isaiah 6:1-8; and Jeremiah 1:4-8.

Fruit to Go—Take a trip to a local grocery store and let kids each pick out one piece of fruit to buy. Return to your meeting place and have kids each relate why they chose their particular piece of fruit. Then discuss the benefits of each fruit of the Spirit as listed in Galatians 5:22-23.

Perfect Protection—Since our society often talks about con-

MEETINGS AND MORE

doms as a means of "protection," take advantage of this opportunity to discuss God's idea of protection. Discuss sexual abstinence before marriage as well as the other types of protection God offers us from the negative effects of our culture.

More of Paul's Advice—Do a book study of one of Paul's letters. You can choose anything from Philemon, with one chapter and one simple message, to Romans, a theological treatise with 16 chapters. Study a chapter or less at each session, and help kids draw out what's most relevant to them.

Table Talk—Use the Table Talk handout (p. 18) as the basis for a meeting with parents and teenagers. During the meeting, have parents and kids complete the handout and discuss it. Encourage families to use the Table Talk handout as a launching pad for a family study of one or more of Paul's letters. Suggest that families begin with a smaller book such as Philippians or Ephesians, and focus on passages that relate to family life. At some point in the meeting, have parents and kids pray together that God would help them all learn to apply Paul's advice in their families.

PARTY PLEASER

Holy Spirit's Fruit Party—Have a party centered on the fruit of the Spirit. Make up fruit-shaped nametags and write the name of the various fruits of the Spirit on them. Have kids act in accordance with the fruit on their nametag. Switch fruit tags every 15 minutes so kids can practice the various attitudes. Serve only fruit and fruit juices. Try some exotic fruit for fun. Discuss which fruits of the Spirit are hardest and which are easiest to grow.

RETREAT IDEA

On the Road With Paul—Base a retreat on some of Paul's travels in the book of Acts. Re-enact some of the exciting events listed here:
    The Stoning of Stephen—Acts 7:54—8:1
    Paul's Conversion—Acts 9:1-19
    Stoned!—Acts 14:8-20
    Freed by an Angel—Acts 16:16-34
    Raising the Dead—Acts 20:7-12
    Shipwrecked!—Acts 27:13-44
    Preaching Jesus Christ—Acts 28:23-30

After each enactment, discuss the effect the event had on Paul's life and his faith in God. Examine how we can learn from Paul's example and his experience. Tie in some of Paul's teachings from this course.

Have kids sleep in tents (Paul was a tent maker) and take long hikes (Paul likely walked many hundreds of miles on his missionary journeys). For fun, give everyone a special "Paul's friend" name for the retreat. Many of Paul's friends are listed in the farewell sections of his letters.

CURRICULUM REORDER—TOP PRIORITY

Order now to prepare for your upcoming Sunday school classes, youth ministry meetings, and weekend retreats! Each book includes all teacher and student materials—plus photocopiable handouts—for any size class!

FOR JUNIOR HIGH/MIDDLE SCHOOL:

Accepting Others: Beyond Barriers & Stereotypes
ISBN 1-55945-126-2

Advice to Young Christians: Exploring Paul's Letters
ISBN 1-55945-146-7

Applying the Bible to Life, ISBN 1-55945-116-5

Becoming Responsible, ISBN 1-55945-109-2

Bible Heroes: Joseph, Esther, Mary & Peter
ISBN 1-55945-137-8

Boosting Self-Esteem, ISBN 1-55945-100-9

Building Better Friendships, ISBN 1-55945-138-6

Can Christians Have Fun?, ISBN 1-55945-134-3

Caring for God's Creation, ISBN 1-55945-121-1

Christmas: A Fresh Look, ISBN 1-55945-124-6

Competition, ISBN 1-55945-133-5

Dealing With Death, ISBN 1-55945-112-2

Dealing With Disappointment, ISBN 1-55945-139-4

Doing Your Best, ISBN 1-55945-142-4

Drugs & Drinking, ISBN 1-55945-118-1

Evil and the Occult, ISBN 1-55945-102-5

Genesis: The Beginnings, ISBN 1-55945-111-4

Guys & Girls: Understanding Each Other
ISBN 1-55945-110-6

Handling Conflict, ISBN 1-55945-125-4

Heaven & Hell, ISBN 1-55945-131-9

Is God Unfair?, ISBN 1-55945-108-4

Love or Infatuation?, ISBN 1-55945-128-9

Making Parents Proud, ISBN 1-55945-107-6

Making the Most of School, ISBN 1-55945-113-0

Materialism, ISBN 1-55945-130-0

The Miracle of Easter, ISBN 1-55945-143-2

Miracles!, ISBN 1-55945-117-3

Peace & War, ISBN 1-55945-123-8

Peer Pressure, ISBN 1-55945-103-3

Prayer, ISBN 1-55945-104-1

Reaching Out to a Hurting World, ISBN 1-55945-140-8

Sermon on the Mount, ISBN 1-55945-129-7

Suicide: The Silent Epidemic, ISBN 1-55945-145-9

Telling Your Friends About Christ, ISBN 1-55945-114-9

The Ten Commandments, ISBN 1-55945-127-0

Today's Faith Heroes, ISBN 1-55945-141-6

Today's Media: Choosing Wisely, ISBN 1-55945-144-0

Today's Music: Good or Bad?, ISBN 1-55945-101-7

What Is God's Purpose for Me?, ISBN 1-55945-132-7

What's a Christian?, ISBN 1-55945-105-X

FOR SENIOR HIGH:

1 & 2 Corinthians: Christian Discipleship
ISBN 1-55945-230-7

Angels, Demons, Miracles & Prayer, ISBN 1-55945-235-8

Changing the World, ISBN 1-55945-236-6

Christians in a Non-Christian World
ISBN 1-55945-224-2

Christlike Leadership, ISBN 1-55945-231-5

Communicating With Friends, ISBN 1-55945-228-5

Counterfeit Religions, ISBN 1-55945-207-2

Dating Decisions, ISBN 1-55945-215-3

Dealing With Life's Pressures, ISBN 1-55945-232-3

Deciphering Jesus' Parables, ISBN 1-55945-237-4

Exodus: Following God, ISBN 1-55945-226-9

Exploring Ethical Issues, ISBN 1-55945-225-0

Faith for Tough Times, ISBN 1-55945-216-1

Forgiveness, ISBN 1-55945-223-4

Getting Along With Parents, ISBN 1-55945-202-1

Getting Along With Your Family, ISBN 1-55945-233-1

The Gospel of John: Jesus' Teachings
ISBN 1-55945-208-0

Hazardous to Your Health: AIDS, Steroids & Eating Disorders, ISBN 1-55945-200-5

Is Marriage in Your Future?, ISBN 1-55945-203-X

Jesus' Death & Resurrection, ISBN 1-55945-211-0

The Joy of Serving, ISBN 1-55945-210-2

Knowing God's Will, ISBN 1-55945-205-6

Life After High School, ISBN 1-55945-220-X

Making Good Decisions, ISBN 1-55945-209-9

Money: A Christian Perspective, ISBN 1-55945-212-9

Movies, Music, TV & Me, ISBN 1-55945-213-7

Overcoming Insecurities, ISBN 1-55945-221-8

Psalms, ISBN 1-55945-234-X

Real People, Real Faith, ISBN 1-55945-238-2

Responding to Injustice, ISBN 1-55945-214-5

Revelation, ISBN 1-55945-229-3

School Struggles, ISBN 1-55945-201-3

Sex: A Christian Perspective, ISBN 1-55945-206-4

Today's Lessons From Yesterday's Prophets
ISBN 1-55945-227-7

Turning Depression Upside Down, ISBN 1-55945-135-1

What Is the Church?, ISBN 1-55945-222-6

Who Is God?, ISBN 1-55945-218-8

Who Is Jesus?, ISBN 1-55945-219-6

Who Is the Holy Spirit?, ISBN 1-55945-217-X

Your Life as a Disciple, ISBN 1-55945-204-8

Order today from your local Christian bookstore, or write: Group Publishing, Box 485, Loveland, CO 80539.

PUT FAITH INTO ACTION...

...with Group's **Projects With a Purpose™ for Youth Ministry.**

Want to try something different with your 7th-12th grade classes? Group's **Projects With a Purpose™ for Youth Ministry** offers four-week courses that really get kids into their faith. Each **Project With a Purpose** course gives you tools to facilitate a project that will provide a direct, purposeful learning experience. Teenagers will discover something significant about their faith while learning the importance of working together, sharing one another's troubles, and supporting one another in love...plus they'll have lots of fun!

Use for Sunday school classes, midweek meetings, home Bible studies, youth groups, retreats, or any time you want to help teenagers discover more about their faith. Your kids will learn more about each other. They'll practice the life skill of working together. And you'll be rewarded with the knowledge that you're providing a life-changing, faith-building experience for your church's teenagers.

Acting Out Jesus' Parables
Strengthen your teenagers' faith as they are challenged to understand the parables' descriptions of the Christian life. Explore such key issues as the value of humility, the importance of hope, and the relative unimportance of wealth.   ISBN 1-55945-147-5

Celebrating Christ With Youth-Led Worship
Kids love to celebrate. Birthdays. Dating. A new car. For Christians, Jesus is the ultimate reason to celebrate. And as kids celebrate Jesus, they'll grow closer to him—an excitement that will be shared with the whole congregation.   ISBN 1-55945-410-5

Checking Your Church's Pulse
Your teenagers will find new meaning for their faith and build greater appreciation for their church with this course. Interviews with congregational members will help your teenagers, and your church, grow closer together.   ISBN 1-55945-408-3

Serving Your Neighbors
Strengthen the "service heart" in your teenagers and watch as they discover the joy and value of serving. Your teenagers will appreciate the importance of serving others as they follow Jesus' example.   ISBN 1-55945-406-7

Sharing Your Faith Without Fear
Teenagers don't have to be great orators to share with others what God's love means to them. With this course, teenagers learn to express their faith through everyday actions without fear of rejection.   ISBN 1-55945-409-1

Teaching Teenagers to Pray
Watch as your teenagers develop strong, effective prayer lives as you introduce them to the basics of prayer. As teenagers explore the depth and excitement of real prayer, they'll learn how to pray with and for others.   ISBN 1-55945-407-5

Teenagers Teaching Children
Teach your teenagers how to share the Gospel with children. Through this course, your teenagers will learn more about their faith by teaching others, plus they'll learn lessons about responsibility and develop teaching skills to last a lifetime.   ISBN 1-55945-405-9

Videotaping Your Church Members' Faith Stories
Teenagers will enjoy learning about their congregation—and become players in their church's faith story with this exciting video project. And, they'll learn the depth and power of God's faithfulness to his people.   ISBN 1-55945-239-0

MORE INNOVATIVE RESOURCES FOR YOUR YOUTH MINISTRY

The Youth Worker's Encyclopedia of Bible-Teaching Ideas: Old Testament/ New Testament

Explore the most comprehensive idea-books available for youth workers! Discover more than 360 creative ideas in each of these 416-page encyclopedias—there's at least one idea for each and every book of the Bible. Find ideas for...retreats and overnighters, learning games, adventures, special projects, parties, prayers, music, devotions, skits, and much more!

Plus, you can use these ideas for groups of all sizes in any setting. Large or small. Sunday or mid-week meeting. Bible study. Sunday school class or retreat. Discover exciting new ways to teach each book of the Bible to your youth group.

Old Testament   ISBN 1-55945-184-X
New Testament   ISBN 1-55945-183-1

Clip-Art Cartoons for Churches

Here are over 180 funny, photocopiable illustrations to help you jazz up your calendars, newsletters, posters, fliers, transparencies, postcards, business cards, announcements—all your printed materials! These fun, fresh illustrations cover a variety of church and Christian themes, including church life, Sunday school, youth groups, school life, sermons, church events, volunteers, and more! And there's a variety of artistic styles to choose from so each piece you create will be unique and original.

Each illustration is provided in the sizes you need most, so it's easy to use. You won't find random images here...each image is a complete cartoon. And these cartoons are fun! In fact, they're so entertaining that you may just find yourself reading the book and not photocopying them at all.

Order your copy of **Clip-Art Cartoons for Churches** today...and add some spice to your next printed piece.

ISBN 1-55945-791-0

Bore No More! (For Every Pastor, Speaker, Teacher)

This book is a must for every pastor, youth leader, teacher, and speaker. These 70 audience-grabbing activities pull listeners into your lesson or sermon—and drive your message home!

Discover clever object lessons, creative skits, and readings. Music and celebration ideas. Affirmation activities. All the innovative techniques 85 percent of adult churchgoers say they wish their pastors would try! (recent Group Publishing poll)

Involve your congregation in the learning process! These complete 5- to 15-minute activities highlight common New Testament Lectionary passages, so you'll use this book week after week.

ISBN 1-55945-266-8